The Armada
Horse and Pony
Quiz Book No. 2

This Armada book belongs to:

# The Armada Horse and Pony Quiz Book No. 2

Charlotte Popescu

Armada

*The Armada Horse and Pony Quiz Book No. 2*
First published in 1974 in Armada by Fontana Paperbacks,
14 St. James's Place, London SW1A 1PF

Reprinted and updated 1978

© Charlotte Popescu 1974

Printed in Great Britain by
Love & Malcomson Ltd., Brighton Road,
Redhill, Surrey

# 1. In Front of the Judges

Can you spot eight differences in these two pictures?

## 2. A Quick Quiz

1. Name five articles of the grooming kit

2. What is the best form of bulk food?

3. What is the name given to a colt or filly between one and two years old?

4. Under B.S.J.A. rules, how many faults are collected for running out in a show jumping competition?

5. Can you think of a four-letter horsy word beginning with R and containing an N?

6. Where is the croup?

7. How many hands high is a horse measuring 64 inches at the withers?

8. Solve the anagram: DIGRIN

9. What is the proper name for the horse's left front leg?

10. To what part of man's body does the horse's knee correspond?

## 3. Points to Remember

When following hounds:

1. Never leave – – – – – open

2. Say – – – – – – – – – – – to the – – – – – on arriving
   at the meet

3. Put a – – – – – – – – – on your pony's tail if he kicks

When jumping:

4. Look – – – – – when going over the jump

5. In the ring always go through the – – – – – and
   – – – – – –

6. Never look – – – – at the fence

When on the road:

7. Lead your pony along the road keeping yourself
   between the – – – – – – – and the pony

8. The most important point is that you must always be
   under complete – – – – – – –

9. When in a group always ride in – – – – – – – – – –

10. Always – – – – – everybody who is helpful

## 4. Crossword

### Across
1. Mountain and – – – – – – – – breeds (8)
5. Ready, steady – – (2)
6. Disease found in the foot (6)
9. Rarely fed to horses (4)
11. A stubborn horse tends to do this (3)
13. We have them too (4)
14. You may ride this way in the saddle (4)
15. The horse – – – his oats (3)

### Down
1. Wild American horses (8)
2. A hedge with a pole on one side (4)
3. May be fed as gruel or tea (7)
4. Slang for horse (3)
7. Get – – (2)
8. Fed in winter (3)
10. You should ride with an independent one (4)
12. Fox's foot (3)

# 5. Who's Who?

Who are, or were, the following:

**1.** The Duke of Beaufort

    (a) A racehorse
    (b) Owner of Badminton
    (c) Master of the Royal Stable

**2.** John Whitaker

    (a) An international showjumper
    (b) An author of horsy books
    (c) Famous horse dealer

**3.** David Vine

    (a) A racehorse trainer
    (b) A commentator
    (c) David Broome's groom

**4.** Hyperion

    (a) Legendary Greek horse
    (b) Mark Phillips's eventing horse
    (c) A famous racehorse

**5.** Sir Edwin Landseer

    (a) A dressage trainer
    (b) A horse painter
    (c) A rodeo rider

**6.** Goodwill

    (a) Lester Piggot's best racehorse
    (b) Famous Roman horse
    (c) Princess Anne's eventing horse

## 6. Odd One Out

Which of these pictures is the odd one out?

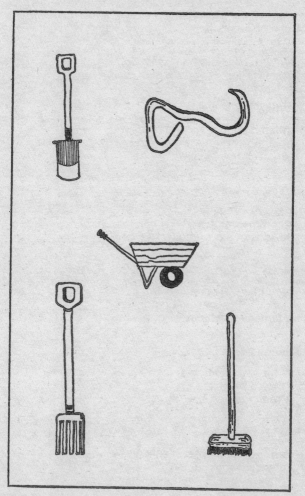

## 7. Pair Them Up

**A.** Can you match these event horses with their riders?

| | | | |
|---|---|---|---|
| 1. Persian Holiday | | a. | Lucinda Prior-Palmer |
| 2. Smokey VI | | b. | Aly Adsett |
| 3. Carawich | | c. | Diane Thorne |
| 4. Kingmaker | | d. | Captain Mark Phillips |
| 5. Killaire | | e. | Richard Meade |
| 6. Jacob Jones | | f. | Chris Collins |

**B.** And these famous horses with their riders?

| | | | |
|---|---|---|---|
| 1. Bucephalus | | a. | Harry M. Llewellyn |
| 2. Marengo | | b. | Pat Taaffe |
| 3. Foxhunter | | c. | Jane Bullen |
| 4. Mancha | | d. | Alexander the Great |
| 5. Arkle | | e. | A. F. Tschiffely |
| 6. Our Nobby | | f. | Napoleon |

## 8. Anagrams

Re-arrange the letters to make ten horsy words

1. LEDVCALEN
2. NEBO ANSVIP
3. MELMOP
4. SNATHNUM
5. SCORS YUNCROT
6. FLANSEF
7. PILECORA
8. GRAMEN
9. HUSPROJD
10. LET RIP

# 9. Training a Young Pony

1. When you are first lunging your pony, should he wear a bit?

2. At about what age should a reasonably mature young pony be backed?

3. What bit should now be used?

4. He must now recover his natural — — — — — — under the weight of his rider

5. When rising at the trot and changing directions, what is it important for you to do?

6. How should you let your pony stretch his neck?

7. It is a good idea to teach your pony to jump down a — — — — — — — — — — —

8. What very useful movement should you teach your pony to make him move away from the leg?

9. When would you use this movement out hacking?

10. What can be done while out hacking to help the pony improve his balance?

11. About what age should your pony be before he can be taken out for a short day's hunting?

12. What is the special name for the enclosure used for the schooling of horses?

## 10. The Saddle

Can you name the different parts of the saddle?

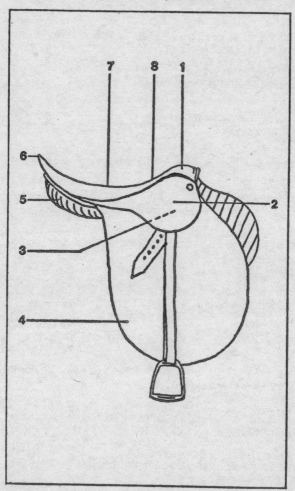

## 11. Ponies in Print

Can you match up the characters with their books and authors?

| Books | Authors |
|---|---|
| 1. Jill and her Perfect Pony | a. Elyne Mitchell |
| 2. Jackie's Pony Patrol | b. Monica Dickens |
| 3. I Rode a Winner | c. Mary Gervaise |
| 4. Follyfoot | d. Christine Pullein-Thompson |
| 5. Silver Brumby | e. Judith Berrisford |
| 6. Ponies and Mysteries | f. Ruby Ferguson |

*Characters*

1. Cobbler

2. Debbie and Cleo

3. Thowra

4. Georgie

5. Jill and Plum

6. Misty

## 12. General Quiz

1. What do you find at Uffington in Berkshire that is to do with horses?

2. What is the average weight of a cart horse?

3. Where is the horse's heart?

4. When is a horse said to be 'aged'?

5. What is a zebroid?

6. Approximately how many times does a horse's pulse beat in one minute?

7. What is a Waler?

8. What is the outside of leather called?

9. What is an elk lip?

10. Give another name for a stable

11. What colour are the wild horses of the Camargue?

12. What is an Onager?

## 13. Crossword

### Across
1. Greek winged horse (7)
5. Dressage tests are performed in these (6)
7. Dorsal or – – – stripe (3)
8. Metal fittings on saddle (2)
9. A jump (5)
10. Tack – – your pony (2)
11. – – the bit (2)
12. A colt is a mare's – – – (3)
14. When the fox is made to change course someone did this (6)

### Down
1. Certain high school movements (7)
2. An inexperienced horse (5)
3. Old line of fox (5)
4. Grooming tool (4)
6. Part of the horse (4)
8. Horse colour (3)
11. This kind of pony needs a lot of care (3)
13. Initials for National Hunt (2)

# 14. Parted Company

These riders have all lost their ponies. Can you follow the routes to discover which pony belongs to which rider?

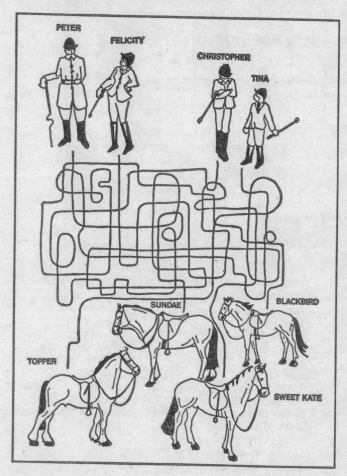

## 15. Bits and Pieces

1. Which way should your horse go when you are lungeing him?

2. Solve the anagram: HYAKMANG

3. Do a horse's teeth grow continually?

4. Solve the half word:

# STRANGLES

5. When is a horse at its prime age?

6. Fill in the missing letters: – o – n e – a – –

7. How many different buckles would you find on a snaffle bridle, including the noseband?

8. Which is the odd one out? Bridoon, weymouth, snaffle, hackamore, kimblewick

9. Call the vet at once if your pony has rubbed his mane and tail. True or false?

10. Solve the anagram: KLABMSTICH

## 16. Blank Verse

Can you complete the lines by filling in the blanks?

1. Your head and your heart keep up!
   Your hands and your − − − − − keep down!
   Your knees press into your horse's side,
   And your − − − − − − into your own.
   (Chijney)

2. Before the gods that made the gods
   Had seen the sunrise pass,
   The white horse of the − − − − −  − − − − −  − − − −
   Was cut out of the − − − − −.
   (G. K. Chesterton)

3. There is no secret so close as that between a − − − − −
   and his horse.
   (R. S. Surtees)

4. 'Bring forth the horse!' The − − − − − was brought;
   In truth, he was a noble − − − − −.
   (Lord Byron)

## 17. Who's the Winner?

Aztec jumped course A, and Benjamin jumped course B. Which horse knocked the most jumps down, and how many faults did they each get?

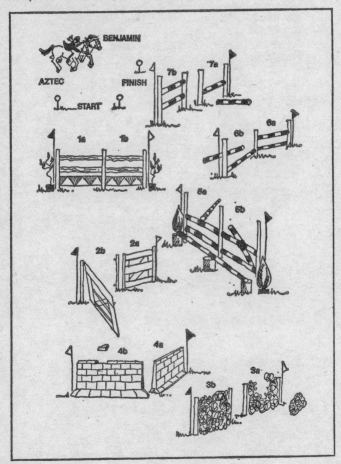

## 18. Where Are They?

1. On what would you find fillet strings?

2. Where would you find the horses of the Household Cavalry?

3. On what would you find a tug and a trace?

4. Where would you find nail-binding?

5. On what would you find a fly-link?

6. In what country would you find a Hanoverian?

7. Where can you find keys and players?

8. Where on the horse would you find a speedy cutting?

9. Where would you find bots?

10. Where would you find the tag of a fox?

11. Where would you find a windgall?

12. In what country would you find an Andalusian?

# 19. Square Words

Can you work out the word in each square by following the letters in a consecutive order?

**1**

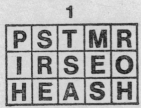

**2**

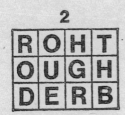

**3**

**4**

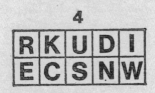

## 20. Hunting Quiz

1. What is a stirrup cup?

2. When does cub hunting start?

3. What is 'lemon-pied'?

4. If hounds are running mute what are they doing?

5. What is a stock?

6. What is meant when hounds 'mark to ground'?

7. What is the foxhunting term for three foxes?

8. What is meant by a foil?

9. Of what is the lash at the end of a hunting whip made?

10. What does 'tally ho over' mean?

11. What is the name given to the floor of hounds kennel courts?

12. What is the name given to someone who rides hard to hounds?

# 21. Crossword

## Across

1. A type of lane used in training (7)
5. – – hounds ran (2)
6. Pain in the belly (5)
7. The legs should look square when this movement is made in a dressage test (4)
9. Lop – – – – (4)
11. The home for a horse (6)
14. A breed of carthorse (5)

## Down

1. Racehorse rider (6)
2. Teeth (6)
3. Sweet – – – –, a skin complaint (4)
4. This injury may be caused by a girth or a saddle (4)
8. Self-inflicted wound on the coronet region (5)
10. Mark on the forehead (4)
12. Abbreviation for black (2)
13. Abbreviation for hands high (2)

# 22. How's your Spelling?

Which words are spelt incorrectly?

**1.** Clydsdale (draught horse)

**2.** Hipology (the study of horses)

**3.** Resin Back (circus name for bareback riding horses)

**4.** Hame-rein (rein on harness)

**5.** Animalitex (poultice)

**6.** Phaeton (carriage)

**7.** Mahogeny tops (leather tops to hunting boots)

**8.** Cavalletti

**9.** Darly Arabian (one of three horses from which the thoroughbred developed)

**10.** Kochaline (used in cleaning tack)

**11.** Spurier (spur-maker)

**12.** Trakener (cross-country fence)

## 23. Grooming Kit

Can you name the different grooming tools?

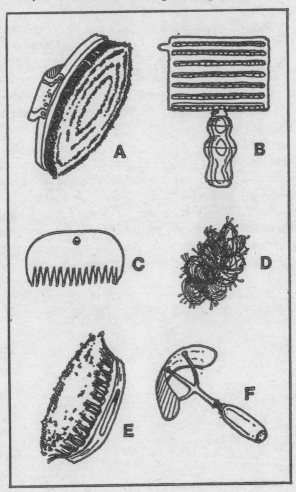

## 24. Story Quiz

What did Paul do wrong?

Paul was going hunting. He caught his pony Moonstone, fed him some nuts, tacked him up and five minutes later was on his way to the meet. Hounds were waiting by a pub. Paul joined them, shouting 'Good morning!' to the huntsman, but at that moment Moonstone started to kick, injuring one of the hounds. The Master called Paul a fool and an idiot. 'You're not fit to hunt,' he shouted. 'Get back to where you belong.'

Later, Paul saw a fox coming out of a covert on the down-wind side. Hoping to redeem his good name, he halloaed with all his might and the fox returned to the covert. Two minutes later the huntsman arrived with hounds in full cry, blowing the gone-away. Then hounds stopped, and the Master shouted, 'You headed the fox, you blithering fool!' and sent Paul home in disgrace.

## 25. Injury Time

1. What is an Animalintex?

2. How would you foment a sprain on a horse's leg?

3. What is an electuary?

4. What are the causes of cracked heels?

5. How would you treat laminitis?

6. What kinds of wounds are kicks and blows?

7. What are the first things you would do to a deep wound found on your horse?

8. How would you treat a girth gall?

9. What is usually applied to most lamenesses causing swelling?

10. If your pony had nail binding, what is the first thing you would do?

11. How would you treat thrush?

12. What is sulphur used for?

29

## 26. Hidden Word

Answer each clue and take a letter from each answer to spell out another horsy word. The letters are in the same position in each word.

**1.** Hot feed made with bran     `_ _ _ _`

**2.** Female horse     `_ _ _ _`

**3.** Coffin bone     `_ _ _ _ _  _ _ _ _`

**4.** . . . . . . Greys are kept at the Royal Mews     `_ _ _ _ _ _ _`

**5.** Strap for keeping rug in place     `_ _ _ _ _ _ _ _ _`

**6.** The 'golden horse of the West'     `_ _ _ _ _ _ _ _`

**7.** Groom at an inn in olden times     `_ _ _ _ _ _`

**8.** To spring up on to a horse from the ground     `_ _ _ _ _`

**9.** Fodder or . . . . . .     `_ _ _ _ _ _`

**10.** A succulent food which is the best of the roots fed to horses     `_ _ _ _ _ _ _`

# 27. Alphabetical Quiz No. 1

A—The purest and most beautiful breed of the equine race

B—The body of the horse from the forearms to the loins

C—The long untidy hairs in the coat after the second clipping

D—A low cart without sides for a heavy load

E—Another name for the dorsal stripe

F—The shaft of a hunting horn

G—South American cowboy

H—Medieval term for a horse

I—Energy from the hocks

J—Small black lumps of grease and dirt found on the saddle

K—A one-reined Pelham with a straight bit and small port

L—A meet at a house by permission of the owner

## 28. Picture Clues

Can you work out the names of some famous horses from the picture clues

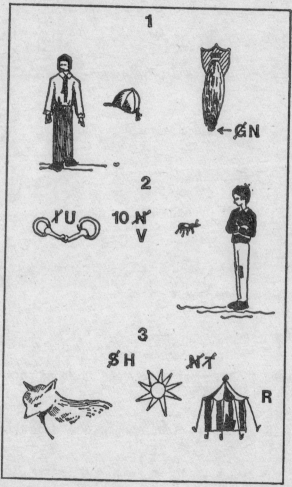

## 29. Famous Horses

1. Where was Dick Turpin going on his famous ride on Black Bess?

2. What was the name of the horse belonging to Thomas Bankes who performed tricks in London in the Elizabethan period?

3. Who won Badminton Horse Trials two years running and the European Championship in 1957 on High and Mighty?

4. What country do brumbies come from?

5. Who was the famous palfrey belonging to Mary Queen of Scots?

6. What was the name of the horse, half brother to the famous showjumper, Foxhunter, ridden many times at the Trooping the Colour?

7. Who now rides Hideaway?

8. Name the favourite racehorse that the Roman Emperor Caligula appointed senator

9. What was the name of the horse belonging to the film star cowboy Roy Rogers?

10. Who rides George, a famous event-horse?

## 30. The Bridle

Can you name all the different parts of the bridle?

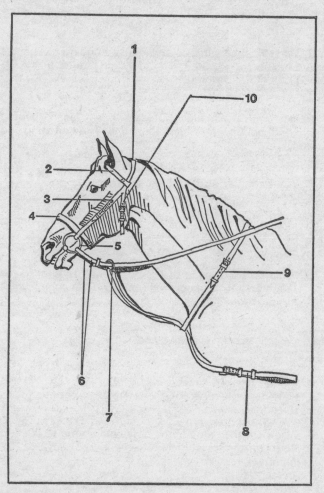

## 31. Crossword

*Across*
1. You may be a member of this (8)
5. May be fed as mash (4)
6. Offspring of male donkeys and mares (5)
8. British Horse Society (3)
9. At these stables horses are kept as boarders (6)
12. The age by which a foal will have six unworn milk teeth (4)
14. How you – – – is important in dressage (3)

*Down*
1. Part of the saddle (6)
2. Hammered into the wall of the foot (4)
3. Breeds with a pony's head and a horse's body (4)
4. Cross country jumps (5)
7. We have one too (3)
8. Name given to an extra hunting day (3)
10. Horse doctor (3)
11. Rarely fed to horses (3)
13. – – grass (2)

## 32. The Long and the Short of It

**1.** Put in the right order from largest to smallest, taking the average height of each one:

   (a)  Suffolk Punch

   (b)  Shetland

   (c)  Dale

   (d)  Cleveland Bay

   (e)  Shire

**2.** Put these courses in order of distance, from longest to shortest:

   (a)  Derby

   (b)  Cross country at Badminton

   (c)  Grand National

   (d)  The Golden Horseshoe Ride

   (e)  The Oaks

**3.** Put in the right order from lightest to darkest:

   (a)  Bay

   (b)  Fleabitten Grey

   (c)  Blue Roan

   (d)  Chestnut

   (e)  Dapple Grey

# 33. Literary Quiz

1. In the book *National Velvet*, what was the colour of the horse the heroine rode?

2. What legendary horse was the story of *Rockwood* based on?

3. What was the 'Genuine Mexican Plug' in the story by Mark Twain?

4. Who wrote the poem *Jack and his Pony Tom*?

5. In Kipling's story, who was the Maltese Cat?

6. Who were Xerxes and Arterxerxes?

7. Why was Arterxerxes so called?

8. Under what name did C. J. Apperley, a well-known sporting author, write?

9. Where did Tschiffely travel with his two horses, Mancha and Gato, on his epic ride?

10. What were the names of the two carthorses in *Animal Farm*?

11. In which book would you find the horses Merrylegs and Captain?

12. How many horses were involved in *The Charge of the Light Brigade*?

## 34. Pictures into Words

Can you name the two pictures in each case to make up a horsy word?

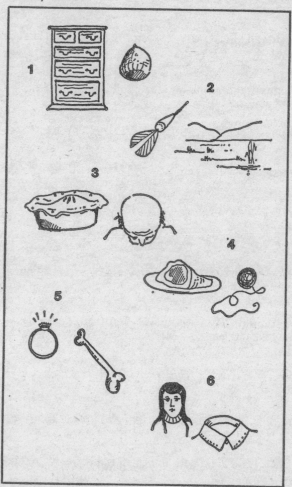

## 35. Horse Doctor

All these items should be kept in a horsy first-aid cupboard. Can you pick out the ones which are being wrongly used?

1. COUGH ELECTUARY used for a horse with a sore throat

2. COMMON SALT used for hardening wounds

3. A ROLL OF GAMGEE TISSUE used for reducing heat

4. WITCH-HAZEL LOTION used for healing wounds

5. OILED SKIN or MACKINTOSH used to protect wound after it has been treated with paste

6. BORACIC POWDER to be put in the foot when a horse has thrush

7. A COLIC DRINK to give to your horse twice a year as a prevention against colic

8. EPSOM SALTS used as a laxative

9. KAOLIN PASTE used when a horse has a cold

10. LEAD LOTION used under a bandage to reduce swelling

## 36. Spot the Pair

Only two pictures are exactly the same. Can you spot them?

## 37. Parts and Points

1. What is a parrot mouth?

2. Where is the haw found on a pony?

3. If the hind leg is 'tied-in' above the hock, what is wrong with it?

4. What is the femur and where would one find it?

5. What is the horse's stifle joint equivalent to on a man?

6. Where is the suspensory ligament?

7. What does 'ram-headed' mean?

8. How many ribs does a horse have?

9. Give another name for the windpipe

10. Which tendon in the hind leg has the most hard-worked muscle?

11. What is the wall of the hoof equivalent to on a man?

12. Where are the sesamoids?

## 38. Mixed Bag

Here the words have been jumbled up, can you unjumble them?

**1.** Him before always pony watering your feed

**2.** Horse too stops head his martingale the high raising a

Here the words are back to front:

**3.** Evig rouy esroh ytnelp fo yah ni retniw

**4.** Kcip tuo ruoy s'ynop sevooh yreve yad

Here both the words and letters are jumbled up in the sentence:

**5.** Aet sehro ton od trawrog uyor etl

Here there is a message in code:

**6.** Whtyen hunttying nevtyer getyt ityn thtye houtynds' watyy

# 39. Join the Dots

Join up the dots to find the pony

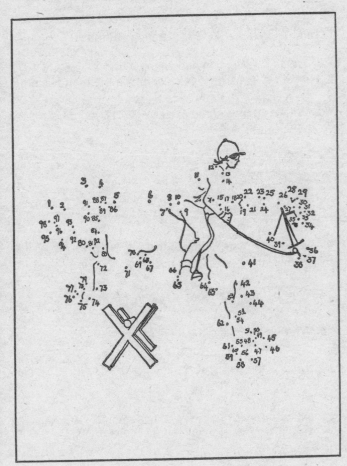

## 40. Who's Who?

**1.** Who is the Patron of Riding For The Disabled?

**2.** Who is the Director of the British Horse Society?

**3.** Which top German showjumper had to retire in 1977 because of a back injury?

**4.** Who is supposed to have said: "A horse! a horse! my kingdom for a horse!"?

**5.** Which top owner and producer of horses owns Penwood Forge Mill?

**6.** Who is the trainer of Red Rum?

**7.** Which famous showjumper is married to David Mould?

**8.** Who is Ireland's top showjumper?

**9.** Who wrote "Black Beauty"?

**10.** What is the name of Harvey Smith's son, a top junior showjumper?

**11.** Who is David Broome's showjumping sister, and to which famous showjumper is she married?

**12.** Which member of the Royal family competes in driving competitions?

## 41. Crossword

**Across**
1. Tack (8)
4. Second thigh (6)
6. – – – – holloa (4)
7. Hay comes in one of these (4)
9. You will have to wear one of these in a class at a show (6)
10. Can be a bang, a switch, or docked (4)
11. Type of riding stick (4)

**Down**
1. This may be a bog or a bone one (6)
2. The huntsman will – – – – a hound from the pack (4)
3. Overhanging upper lip (3)
4. A kind of snaffle (6)
5. An – – – pony will probably have a staring coat (3)
7. A wager on a race-horse (3)
8. A beautiful breed (4)

## 42. Horses of Long Ago

1. In medieval times, why did knights have to be hoisted on to their horses by crane?

2. How did Bellerophon tame Pegasus?

3. What was the colour and breed of Napoleon's charger Marengo?

4. When was the Spanish Riding School founded?
(a) 1735 (b) 1662 (c) 1902

5. Who was Alcock Arabian?

6. What were bearing reins used for?

7. About how long ago did Eohippus, the ancestor of the horse, live?

8. What is a destrier?

9. Where do the wild Przevalski horses live?

10. What was the name of the Duke of Wellington's horse?

11. About what time in English history did fox hunting become truly established?

12. What are tarpans?

## 43. Adding On

Can you add on some letters to these half words to make new horsy words?

**1.** Two words beginning with HACK

**2.** Four words beginning with BAR

**3.** Two words beginning with CAN

**4.** Three words beginning with BUCK

**5.** Four words beginning with FOR

**6.** Two words beginning with PAL

**7.** Two words beginning with WIND

**8.** Two words beginning with NEW

## 44. Yes or No

1. Is a 'stake and bind' a kind of fence?

2. Did Point to Points originate from riding from one steeple to another?

3. Is the correct place to start grooming on the off side starting with the legs?

4. Do beagles hunt foxes?

5. Did Xenophon write books on equitation?

6. Do hounds smell foxes? (Is this the right expression to use?)

7. Does a gag snaffle act on the corners of the lips?

8. Is the half pass a lateral movement?

9. Does every Pony Club have its own. hunt?

10. Do hock boots protect the hocks when travelling?

11. Is Fernie a kind of hunting horn?

12. Are cracked heels caused by neglecting to dry the legs after washing?

## 45. Name the Markings

Can you name all the horse markings in the pictures?

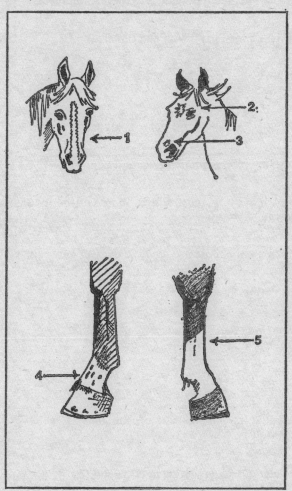

## 46. Mountain and Moorland Breeds

**1.** Name the nine mountain and moorland breeds.

**2.** Where does the native Fell pony live?

**3.** What is the characteristic feature in the appearance of the Exmoor pony?

**4.** What were the Fell and Dale ponies used for years ago?

**5.** About what height is a Shetland pony?

**6.** Which is the biggest and strongest of the mountain and moorland breeds?

**7.** What are the most usual colours of Dartmoor ponies?

**8.** Name the three different types of Welsh ponies

**9.** What was the Shetland pony used for before becoming a riding pony?

**10.** Where is the native land of the Highland pony?

**11.** Which breed is considered the most popular and beautiful?

**12.** What is the most predominant colour of the Connemara?

## 47. Picture Pairs

Which items go together?

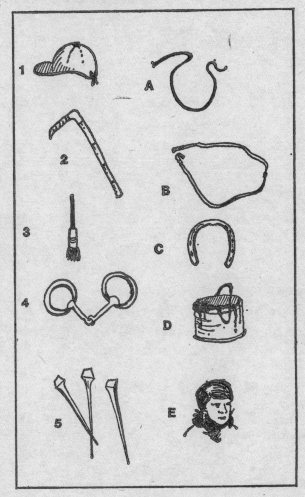

## 48. Synonyms

Can you think of another word for each of the following?

1. Genet

2. Dorsal stripe

3. Cannon bone

4. Race

5. The fox 'throws his tongue'

6. Strawberry roan

7. Throat lash

8. Pedal bone

9. Founder

10. Renvers

## 49. What's Wrong?

How many things is the girl doing wrong, and are there any other mistakes in the picture?

## 50. Equitation

**1.** What is the 'time' of the trot?

**2.** When a horse yields its jaw to the bit and bends his neck from the poll, what is he doing?

**3.** On which side should you mount?

**4.** What is an Irish Martingale used for?

**5.** When a horse jibs what does he do?

**6.** What is the best form of stick made from?

**7.** If a horse is splay-footed what will he do when he moves?

**8.** What is the name of the action the jointed snaffle gives?

**9.** For what purpose are gags used? Are they severe?

**10.** Name the term describing a horse which leans too much on the bit.

**11.** What are the main reasons for work on two tracks?

**12.** Name as many different kinds of canters as you can

## 51. One or the Other

In each case, either **a** or **b** is the right answer. Can you tell which?

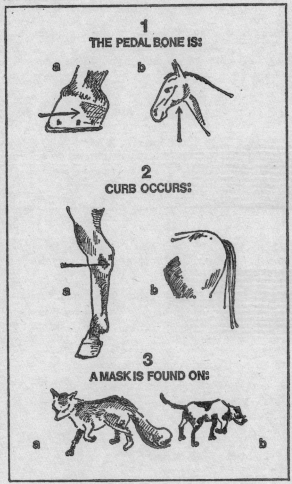

**1**
THE PEDAL BONE IS:

a

b

**2**
CURB OCCURS:

a

b

**3**
A MASK IS FOUND ON:

a

b

## 52. Missing Links

What are the missing words in these sentences?

1. A — — — — —  — — — — — — knot should be used to tie up a pony

2. If you jerk your horse's mouth you are said to — — — the mouth

3. — — — — — — — is the best kind of hay for horses

4. A sharp gallop to clear a horse's wind is called a — — — — — — — — — —

5. A properly bedded down stable is said to be — — — — — — —

6. When riding, you should keep a straight line from your shoulders through your hips to your — — — — —

7. The paved yard in kennels for exercising hounds is called the — — — — —

8. Hard, frosty ground is said to have — — — — in it

9. Horses should not be put in the stable and left — — — — — — — — — after a long ride

10. 'The Great Horse' is a name given to the — — — — — breed

## 53. More Square Words

Discover the horsy words by following the letters round
the boxes

**1**

**2**

**3**

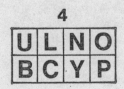

**4**

## 54. The Foot

**1.** Name the different parts of the hoof?

**2.** What is 'dumping'?

**3.** Why can nails be driven through the wall of the hoof without causing pain?

**4.** What is the use of the frog?

**5.** Name the blacksmith's tool used for paring or cutting the hoof back

**6.** What are clips used for?

**7.** How many nails on the inside and how many on the outside of a hunter shoe?

**8.** What is a feather-edged shoe used for?

**9.** Name the reasons why a pony may need reshoeing

**10.** What is the most usual kind of shoe used and why does it have a groove?

**11.** Where would one find a sandcrack, and what is it?

**12.** What are corns?

## 55. Horsy Words

How many horsy words can you make out of:

# MARTINGALE

Each word must contain at least three letters and each letter can only be used once in the same word. (Although A, as it appears twice, may be used twice).

## 56. Crazy Mix-up

Can you unjumble the letters of the words in these sentences? Not all the words are anagrams

1. Gadhilhn ipeson live diwl in catsondl

2. A pirset si a narrow tewhi mark wodn the cafe

3. Spenoi era happier thiw a companion ni eht same dilef.

4. It si a doog idea ot negul a young nopy

5. Sheros are usually donf fo gusra

6. A rohes should ont be dinerd a tegar deal when lony orfu esayr old

7. If oruy npoy teas rogawtr he will die

8. The orculo of a lipabed is clakb nad white

9. A plecipd ehosr should eb lastebd in tewnir

10. A psik can eb edus instead fo a wheelrowbar rof cinugkm out

## 57. What's in a Name?

These three sets of pictures each represent a horsy word
Take the first letter of each name to discover what it is

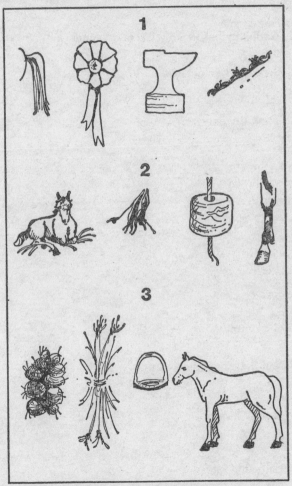

## 58. Foreign Names

Do you know the nationalities of these showjumpers?

1. Fritz Ligges

2. Graziano Mancinelli

3. Frank Chapot

4. Hendrik Snoek

5. Hugo Simon

6. Nelson Pessoa

7. Douglas Bunn

8. Paul Schockemöhle

9. Piero D'Inzeo

10. Sally Mapleson

## 59. Can You Name

**1.** Three colours of horses beginning with B

**2.** Three markings on the head beginning with S

**3.** Two parts of the bridle beginning with B

**4.** Four points of the horse beginning with H

**5.** Three parts of the horse beginning with T

**6.** Two kinds of jumps beginning with R

**7.** Three British breeds of horses or ponies beginning with S

**8.** Three different foods fed to horses beginning with C

**9.** Two items of the grooming kit beginning with W

**10.** Three causes of lameness beginning with S

## 60. Face the Opposition

Do you know the opposites to these horsy words?

**1.** She-ass

**2.** Parrot mouth

**3.** Arve *(Call to turn left)*

**4.** Roach back

**5.** Near

**6.** Entire

**7.** Dish faced

**8.** Bang tail

**9.** Travers

**10.** Posting at the trot

# 61. Poetry Quiz

Do you know where these verses come from? (Give the name of the poem and the poet)

## 1.

'Are you ready for your steeplechase, Lorraine, Lorraine,
   Lorrèe?
You're booked to ride your capping race today at Coulterlee.
You're booked to ride Vindictive, for all the world to see,
To keep him straight, and keep him first, and win the run
   for me.'
She clasped her new-born baby, poor Lorraine, Lorraine,
   Lorrèe.
'I cannot ride Vindictive, as any man can see,
And I will not ride Vindictive, with this baby on my knee;
He's killed a boy, he's killed a man, and why must he kill
   me?'
She mastered young Vindictive — Oh! the gallant lass was
   she,
And kept him straight and won the race as near as near
   could be;
But he killed her at the brook against a pollard willow tree,
Oh! he killed her at the brook, the brute, for all the world
   to see,
And no one but the baby cried for poor Lorraine, Lorraine,
   Lorrèe.

## 2.

'Bring forth the horse!' — the horse was brought;
In truth, he was a noble steed,
A tartar of the Ukraine breed,
Who look'd as though the speed of thought
Were in his limbs; but he was wild,
Wild as the deer, and untaught,
With spur and bridle undefiled —
'Twas but a day he had been caught.

c

## 62. How Many?

**1.** Clips on a hind shoe?

**2.** Wheels on a phaeton?

**3.** Incisor teeth in a horse?

**4.** Rings on a standing martingale?

**5.** Wheels on a hansom cab?

**6.** Ergots on a horse?

**7.** Buckles on a noseband?

**8.** Inches in 16·3 hands?

**9.** Whipper-ins (usually) assisting a huntsman?

**10.** Reins on a kimblewick?

**11.** Feet in the length of a large dressage arena?

**12.** Miles in the 1,000 and 2,000 Guineas at Newmarket?

## 63. Racing Quiz

1. Which are the five Classic races?

2. In which year was the Derby first run?

3. Which king is sometimes referred to as the father of racing?

4. Why did Arkle have to retire?

5. At about what speed do most racehorses gallop?

6. Where is Tattenham Corner?

7. How many times has Red Rum won the Grand National?

8. What are racing colours?

9. Racehorses all have their birthdays on the same day. What date is this?

10. At about what speed is the Derby run?

11. Which horse won the Cheltenham Gold Cup in 1976?

12. Which jockey rode this horse?

## 64/65. Giant Crossword

*Across*

1. A contagious infection of the nose and throat (9)
6. You may rise or do this at the trot (3)
8. This is done on the forehand or on the haunches (4)
9. Used to keep the rug in place (6)
12. Blacksmith's hoof-filing tools (5)
15. Wounds on the coronet (6)
16. Horse noise (5)
18. Poetical name for a horse (5)
20. British Horse Society (3)
22. – – – – pegging: mounted game played by the British Cavalry especially in India (4)
23. Kind of brush (5)
27. Keeps the saddle on (5)
29. Compartments in which horses are haltered (6)
30. An Exmoor pony has this sort of nose (5)

*Down*

1. Breed of carthorse (5)
2. Post and – – – – (4)
3. Part of the horse's head (4)
4. Your stable should always be – – – -fair (3)
5. Tied round the neck for small children to hold on to when jumping (5)
7. You ride with your feet in these (5)
10. A high school movement (6)
11. Give a horse medicine using a bottle (6)
13. Marking on the head (4)
14. A gait (4)
17. What you pay a cap to do (4)
18. Often describes a fox (3)
19. A horse colour (3)
20. A more common colour (3)
21. Marking on the face (6)
24. One of the oldest breeds (4)
25. A native breed (4)
26. Relation of the horse (3)
28. Most common form of bulk food (3)

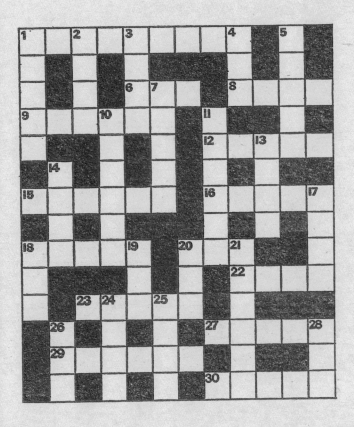

## 66. What are they?

Can you name all these articles?

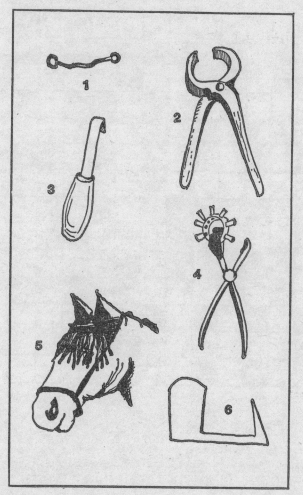

## 67. Half and Half

Pick the right words from below to complete the horsy phrases

1. FLYING .........

2. ......... MEET

3. OVER .........

4. ......... CLOSED

5. FULL .........

6. ......... SEAT

7. STIRRUP .........

8. ......... FACE

9. DROP .........

10. ......... GALL

11. NECK .........

12. ...... GUARD

RACING STRAP TREAD FACED FENCE CHANGE
TAIL MOUTH GIRTH ROAD OPENING WHITE

## 68. Spot the Pair

Only two pictures are exactly the same. Can you spot them?

# 69. General Quiz

1. What is a fiddle head?

2. Which horses are usually known as cold blooded?

3. What is another name for studs which prevent a horse slipping?

4. If you were given the 'latchfords' what would you be receiving?

5. What is meant by 'poached'?

6. Pure mountain and moorland breeds are registered in what book?

7. How do you quarter a horse?

8. What are soup-plates?

9. What is the name of the 'wheel' that one can find at the head of a spur?

10. How is a wisp made?

11. What one word refers to a horse's make and shape?

12. What is a skeleton-break?

## 70. Mixed Doubles

Can you sort out these half words to make horsy words?

1. BROW MOOR
   PAD HUNT
   FOX DOCK
   STRING BALD
   PIE BAND
   FORE HALT
   DART LOCK

2. HIGH FINCH
   DRESS SMITH
   SAND KIN
   BULL LAND
   NOSE CRACK
   BLACK AGE
   GAS BAND

## 71. Crossword

*Across*
1. Pony – – – – – – – – is a popular holiday occupation (8)
5. Old term for a saddle horse (3)
6. Its condition is always a good indication of a horse's health (4)
8. Race run at Epsom (4)
10. A nutritious food (4)
11. Male horse under four years old (4)
13. A pace (4)
14. May be a night or a day one (3)

*Down*
1. Part of the horse's leg (6)
2. Growth at back of fetlock joints (5)
3. A vice (4)
4. Often jumped (5)
7. Inn's groom (6)
9. Racecourse (5)
12. Abbreviation for brown (2)

## 72. Odd Items Out

Can you pick out the items you definitely do not need for cleaning your tack?

SPONGE

MANE COMB

SADDLE HORSE

KOCHOLINE

TIN OF BRASS POLISH

WISP

BUCKET

CHAMOIS LEATHER

HOOKS

KNIFE

METAL POLISH

DANDY BRUSH

WASHING UP LIQUID

OLD CLOTH

COOKING OIL

DUSTER

SADDLE SOAP

STABLE RUBBER

## 73. Name the Plants

Can you name these plants which are poisonous to horses?

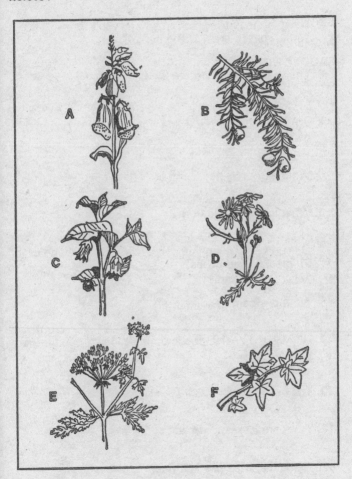

## 74. Western Riding

1. Which American breed is considered the most popular?

2. What is the name given to a pony used for separating cattle from the rest of the herd?

3. The walk and the jog are the first two paces—what is the third?

4. What are the kind of riding trousers used by cowboys called?

5. What is the Western term for a girth?

6. What is the saddle horn?

7. Do you know the name of the rawhide noseband used for breaking purposes?

8. What is a paint gelding?

9. What is the characteristic of an American saddle-bred horse?

10. The British say hogged. The Americans say – – – – – – – –

11. What are jack-knifing and sunfishing?

12. Name the lasso used by riders to catch steer

# 75. Horse-words

Do you know the correct definitions of these words?

1. JENNY
   (a) Famous racehorse
   (b) Female donkey
   (c) Two-wheeled pony trap
   (d) Side-saddle horse

2. KNABSTRUP
   (a) Danish breed of horse
   (b) Military saddle
   (c) Horse that rears
   (d) German lasso

3. MANGE
   (a) Horse colour between grey and dun
   (b) Untidy horse
   (c) Small manger
   (d) Skin disease

4. POULTICE
   (a) Feed made of linseed and bran
   (b) Warm paste applied to an infected part
   (c) Infected foot
   (d) Rogue pony

5. TERRETS
   (a) Polo sticks
   (b) Dividing rails in a horse box
   (c) Kinds of jump
   (d) Part of horse's harness

6. SITFAST
   (a) Dressage movement
   (b) Swelling on the horse
   (c) Bronco buster
   (d) Contagious disease

## 76. Quick Quote Quiz

Who said or wrote the following?

1. 'Three jolly gentlemen
   In coats of red,
   Rode their horses up to bed.'

2. 'Four things greater than all things are women, horses, power and war.'

3. 'And I saw, and behold a white horse: and he that sat on him had a bow: and a crown was given unto him: and he went forth conquering, and to conquer.'

4. 'A grain which in England is generally given to horses, but in Scotland supports the people.'

5. 'The 'oss loves the 'ound and I loves both.'

## 77. Odd Picture Out

Which of these pictures is the odd one out?

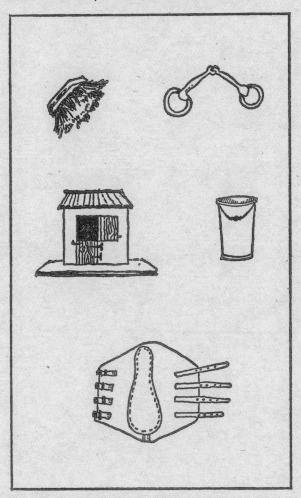

## 78. Missing Letters

1. F – T L – – –

2. – I P – Z – A N – –

3. – A – T – N G – – E

4. C – P R – – L E

5. – H O – – U – P – N –

6. – K – W – A L –

7. – R – N D N – – I – N – L

8. P – L – – I – O

9. H – R – E S –

10. T – O T – I – G

11. – A – – L – E T – I

12. – R E – D I – –

## 79. Crossword

### Across

1. – – – – jumping (4)
3. Jockey's headgear (3)
5. Teeth (8)
7. – – – ponies work in mines (3)
8. Part of the horse (5)
9. Hounds are – – blood when they have recently killed (2)
10. The handle of a hunting whip can be made from this (4)
11. Pole, rail or – – – (3)

### Down

1. Kind of hay (8)
2. Horse noise (6)
3. Incorrect term for a whip (4)
4. – – – – and rails (4)
6. Kind of school (6)
10. Abbreviation for brown (2)

# 80. Ailments

**1.** What are the symptoms of navicular?

**2.** Where is sidebone found?

**3.** Give another name for a capped elbow

**4.** Why did a thorough-pin used to be called a through-pin?

**5.** What is poll evil?

**6.** How is azoturia caused?

**7.** Name the nervous disease in which the hock is jerked upwards

**8.** What is the most common skin complaint of the pony?

**9.** Where on the horse are warbles found?

**10.** What is a rope gall?

**11.** If your horse makes a noise when galloping and has an infection of the larynx, what is this called?

**12.** Where does mallenders, an inflammation of the skin, occur?

## 81. More Mistakes

In this story quiz, what did Jill and her parents do wrong?

'I want a pony at once,' Jill said. 'It's my birthday in three days and you promised me one as a present, Daddy.'

'All right then; we'll go to the horse sale the day after tomorrow. There are two hundred horses to choose from, so we're certain to find something suitable,' replied her father.

The sale was held in a large covered building. Jill chose a small dappled grey pony.

'I've always wanted a grey. I shall call him Cavalier,' she said.

The catalogue described him as a three-year-old of twelve hands two inches. He was 'knocked down' to Jill's father for one hundred pounds. The same evening he was delivered by horse box. Jill wanted to ride him at once. She was not very experienced, but she had had some riding lessons and could canter. A friend had lent her a set of tack. So five minutes after the arrival of Cavalier, she was mounting in the back yard. She sat down firmly in the saddle and picked up the reins. She pushed Cavalier with her legs, but he refused to walk forward. Her father handed her a riding stick, but when she hit him, he ran backwards faster and faster until he was against the yard wall. Then he reared. Jill screamed and pulled frantically on the reins. He lost his balance and fell. Jill was underneath, crushed against the wall.

Cavalier stood up first and cantered away. Jill got slowly to her feet. Her arm was broken.

## 82. Showjumpers

Who rides the following horses?

**1.** Philco

**2.** Penwood Forge Mill

**3.** Marius

**4.** Moxy

**5.** Graffiti

**6.** Kerry Gold

**7.** Miniature

**8.** Everest Maleedi

**9.** Law Court

**10.** Double Brandy

## 83. Join the Dots

Join up the dots to find what the horse is doing

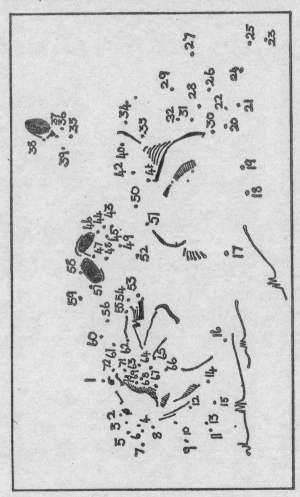

## 84. Jumping

1. Can you name the main reasons for elimination in a showjumping event?

2. When a horse is landing over a jump what should his head and neck do?

3. How much money has a Grade 'B' horse won?

4. Approximately when did Caprilli introduce the forward seat?

5. Who used to ride Doublet?

6. How far from the jump should a horse take off?

7. What are Foxhunter jumping competitions, and after whom are these competitions named?

8. Who designs the courses at Hickstead?

9. Should you ride quite slowly or quite fast at parallel bars?

10. What event is held at Tidworth every year?

11. How does a double oxer differ from an ordinary oxer?

12. What is meant by 'rapping'?

## 85. Special Mixture

*Art*

1. Who is the most famous of horse painters?

2. For what kind of painting were the Alkens famous?

3. Name the well-known horse painter Sir Alfred James
   M – – – – – – –

*Gymkhanas*

4. What would you do in the event 'Drum Elimination'?

5. Who won the Prince Philip Cup in 1973?

6. Do you have to be under a certain age to gymkhana?

*Polo*

7. How long is a chukka?

8. What is the correct term for a polo stick?

9. Approximately when was polo introduced to Britain?

10. How long is a polo ground?

## 86. Yes or No

1. Are 'oyster feet' flattish hooves marked with ridges?

2. Are brass hunt buttons worn with a scarlet coat?

3. Does the expression 'hound pace' refer to the speed at which the pack chases the fox?

4. Is a 'Don' a Russian Steppe horse?

5. Does 'throwing their tongues' mean that hounds are very eager for the fox?

6. Does the throat lash stop the headpiece from being pulled over the head?

7. Is straw the best kind of bedding?

8. Is linseed warmed up before being given to horses?

9. Does 'tied in below the knee' mean the horse's leg is very short below the knee?

10. Is a 'pad' the foot of a fox?

11. Is a horse's mane plaited to improve its condition?

12. Is a troika a Russian term for three horses driven abreast pulling a sleigh?

# 87. Crossword

## Across
1. Keeps the rug in place (6)
5. Might be 'pricked' (3)
6. Kind of spavin (4)
7. Part of the foot (4)
10. American breed (8)
11. A pony may be – – grass (2)
12. Too much of this may cause laminitis (5)

## Down
1. A horse has eight true and ten false ones (4)
2. The last thing a horse will do when jumping (4)
3. Gets back on again (8)
4. There are nine different native ones in Britain (6)
8. It may be a deep or a torn one (3)
9. White marking on forehead (4)
10. The hunting season officially ends on the first of this month (3)

## 88. Initials

What do the following initials stand for?

**1.** N.E.C.

**2.** M.F.H.A.

**3.** N.P.S.

**4.** H.O.Y.S.

**5.** R.C.

**6.** R.D.


Give the recognised abbreviations for the following:

**7.** Black

**8.** Favourite

**9.** Colt

**10.** 14 Hands high

**11.** Thoroughbred

**12.** Fell

## 89. Who Lives Where?

Can you match the breeds to their original homes?
CONNEMARA   EXMOOR   HIGHLAND   FELL
SHETLAND   DARTMOOR

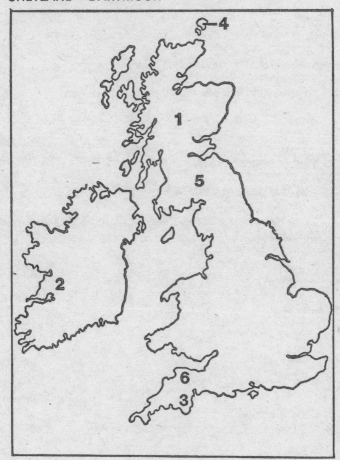

## 90. The Armada Handicap

As the horses thundered past the finishing post, they were placed in the following order. Who would you have put your money on to win, and who came last?

Father's Folly was a nose in front of Oxford Blue

Winalot was three places behind Hurry Harry

Tornado could see seven horses in front of him

Lightning Streak was between Westward Ho and Hurry Harry

Flying Dutchman was second to last

Likely Lad was between Bee Line and Father's Folly

Tornado was two places behind Lightning Streak

Oxford Blue was fourth

# 91. Stable Management

1. What is bran made from?

2. What is a balding girth?

3. Why should barley straw not be used for bedding?

4. What are arched rollers used for?

5. How many pounds does a truss of hay weigh?

6. What are single lamps used for?

7. Can you name three materials from which a bit is made?

8. Why is it not good to feed clover hay?

9. How much coat is taken off when a horse is hunter clipped?

10. What is meant by 'short racking'?

11. What is a Sheringham window?

12. Why is chaff sometimes added to the feed?

## 92. Name the Injuries

Can you name the ailments that would be found at these twelve points?

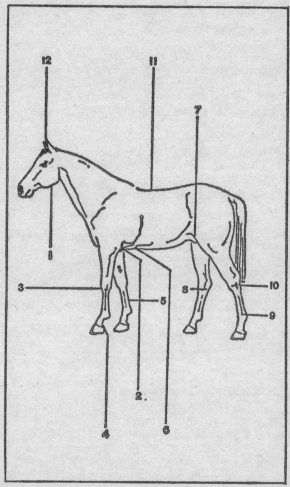

## 93. Across Country

Where are the following British events held every year?

**1.** THE DERBY
    (a) Ascot
    (b) Derby
    (c) Upminster
    (d) Epsom Downs

**2.** BADMINTON THREE-DAY EVENT
    (a) Yorkshire
    (b) Berkshire
    (c) Gloucestershire
    (d) Devon

**3.** POLO CHAMPIONSHIPS
    (a) Cowdray Park
    (b) Sandown Park
    (c) Cheltenham
    (d) Windsor

**4.** THE JUMPING DERBY
    (a) White City
    (b) Burghley
    (c) Hickstead
    (d) Tattersalls

**5.** 1,000 AND 2,000 GUINEAS
    (a) Newmarket
    (b) Aintree
    (c) Goodwood
    (d) Doncaster

**6.** GEORGE V GOLD CUP
    (a) Sandringham
    (b) Olympia
    (c) Haydock
    (d) Wembley

D

## 94. Horse Sense?

These riddles have all got something to do with horses. Can you solve them?

**1.** What has an egg in it which never breaks?

**2.** What hops and is also found in the foot?

**3.** What is standing but has no legs?

**4.** What can never be eaten but often goes stale?

**5.** What are true as well as false?

**6.** What can be ewe but never sheep?

**7.** What can be drawn without pencil or paper?

**8.** What pecks but is not a hen?

**9.** When is a field without any land?

**10.** Where is there posting without any letters?

## 95. Alphabetical Quiz No. 2

M—The cry of the hounds when hunting

N—Name given to the squeezing action of a jointed snaffle

O—Horse of more than two colours

P—Turn on the haunches at the canter

Q—Horse that drops food from its mouth when chewing

R—A blacksmith's tool

S—Bars between which a horse is harnessed

T—Term used to describe a thin horse, when its loins are drawn up behind the ribs

U—A deformity of the horse's jaw, when the lower jaw protrudes beyond the upper

V—Small circle in equitation

W—Unweaned hound puppies

X—One of Mr. Jorrocks' hunters

Y—A horse's action when fighting with its head, reaching outwards and downwards

Z—Striping on the limbs

## 96. Spot the Mistakes

Which pictures have mistakes in them, and what is wrong ?

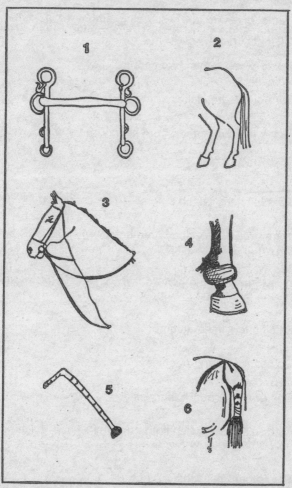

## 97. Records and Feats

Do you know:

1. Who was the first woman to ride for Britain in an Olympic Three-Day Event?

2. Which is the world's largest racecourse?

3. Who was the youngest rider to ever win Badminton?

4. Who was the first woman to win an individual medal for show jumping in the Olympics?

5. The largest number of horses ever to race together in the Grand National?

6. The year when equestrian events were first included in the Olympic Games?

7. The height of the tallest-ever racehorse?

8. The name of the only woman to have won Badminton three times?

9. Who was the first woman to win a team medal for show jumping at the Olympics?

10. The record time for the Derby?

## 98. Double Meaning

Two words have been jumbled together, but the letters are in the right order. Can you sort them out?

**1. SHAINRVEIL**

Take away the cart horse and you are left with a piece of blacksmith's equipment

**2. HCRUNETSINTG**

Take away the sport and you are left with a point of the horse

**3. SMATRNIGEPER**

Take away the marking and you are left with something used for feeding horses

**4. PSAODLDLEORY**

Take away the game and you are left with some tack

**5. RSANAFSFLPE**

Take away the blacksmith's tool and you are left with a kind of bit

**6. DORENACTHS**

Take away the method of giving medicine as a drink and you are left with a feed

## 99. A Rag Man's Anagrams?

If HORSE and SHORE are anagrams of eath other, can you work out more double words from these clues?

1. horse's pace
_ _ _ _ _ _

dreamlike state of mind
_ _ _ _ _ _

2. animals that often get on well with horses
_ _ _ _

what horses do when they lose shoes
_ _ _ _

3. facial marking
_ _ _ _ _

vicar
_ _ _ _ _

4. mounted game
_ _ _ _

coil of rope
_ _ _ _

5. unsound horse
_ _ _ _

time for eating
_ _ _ _

6. trick circus horses learn which is a vice in all others
_ _ _ _

could be used to describe an albino
_ _ _ _

7. moorland breed
_ _ _ _

you'll find the winning racehorse in this place!
_ _ _ _

8. vital part of the saddle
_ _ _ _ _

opposite of left
_ _ _ _ _

9. cow pony's gait
_ _ _ _

simple jump
_ _ _ _

10. style of riding that used to be considered most unladylike
_ _ _ _ _ _ _

raging speeches
_ _ _ _ _ _ _

## 100. Advanced Quiz

1. How many toes had the Eohippus, the ancestor of the horse?

2. What is a Donsky?

3. Where do you take a horse's pulse?

4. How much money has a Grade J.A. pony won?

5. Name the high school movement where the horse, posing at full rear, jumps off its hocks and lands on its hind legs

6. What is a syce?

7. After the Eohippus, there were three more kinds of horse before Equus, the horse of today. Can you name them?

8. What do you understand by a direct flexion?

9. Where are the wolf teeth in a horse's mouth?

10. Who used to ride Vibart?

11. What is the name of the cart used for racing trotters and pacers?

12. What does 'cadence' mean?

**Answers**

**1.** The rosette on the centre cup is different. The head-collar has a ring in the top picture. The right-hand judge has no pocket badge in the top picture. The centre judge's tie is different. The left-hand fence post is different. The handler's turn-up is missing in the bottom picture. The knot in the fence rail is missing in the bottom picture. The right-hand table leg has been altered.

**2.** 1. Dandy brush, body brush, curry comb, water brush, hoof pick, stable rubber, sponge, mane comb, wisp. 2. Hay. 3. Yearling. 4. 3 faults. 5. Rein, roan. 6. The part of the hindquarters between the loins and the tail. 7. 16 hands. 8. Riding. 9. Near fore. 10. Wrist.

**3.** 1. gates. 2. good morning, master. 3. red ribbon. 4. ahead. 5. start, finish. 6. down. 7. traffic. 8. control. 9. single file. 10. thank.

**4.** *Across:* 1. Moorland. 5. Go. 6. Thrush. 9. Peas. 11. Nap. 13. Eyes. 14. Side. 15. Ate.
*Down:* 1. Mustangs. 2. Oxer. 3. Linseed. 4. Nag. 7. Up. 8. Hay. 10. Seat. 12. Pad.

**5.** 1. b. 2. a. 3. b. 4. c. 5. b. 6. c.

**6.** Hoof pick. The others are all used for mucking out the stable.

**7.** A. 1 and d, 2 and f, 3 and b, 4 and c, 5 and a, 6 and e, B. 1 and d, 2 and f, 3 and a, 4 and e, 5 and b, 6 and c.

**8.** 1. Cleveland Bay. 2. Bone Spavin. 3. Pommel. 4. Huntsman. 5. Cross country. 6. Snaffle. 7. Capriole. 8. Manger. 9. Jodhpurs. 10. Triple.

**9.** 1. No, a cavesson (a superior kind of headcollar). 2. At about three years old. 3. A snaffle. 4. Balance. 5. Change your diagonal. 6. By walking him on a loose rein. 7. Jumping lane. 8. Turn on the forehand. 9. When opening a gate, and when riding along the road to keep his quarters in. 10. Riding up and down hills. 11. Four years old. 12. Manege.

**10.** 1. Pommel. 2. Skirt. 3. Stirrup bar. 4. Saddle flap. 5. Panel. 6. Cantle. 7. Seat. 8. Waist.

**11.** 1. Jill and Her Perfect Pony by Ruby Ferguson with Jill and Plum. 2. Jackie's Pony Patrol by Judith Berrisford with Misty. 3. I Rode a Winner by Christine Pullein-Thompson with Debbie and Cleo. 4. Follyfoot by Monica Dickens with Cobbler. 5. Silver Brumby by Elyne Mitchell with Thowra. 6. Ponies and Mysteries by Mary Gervaise with Georgie.

**12.** 1. The famous white horse carved on the hillside. 2. 15 cwt. 3. Behind the elbow. 4. Seven years or older. 5. An animal half zebra, half horse. 6. 36–40 beats a minute. 7. An Australian breed of horse. 8. The grain side. 9. A wide, loose, over-hanging lip. 10. Loose box or shippon. 11. Grey. 12. An ass of Asiatic origin of a refined and racy type.

**13.** *Across:* 1. Pegasus. 5. Arenas. 7. Eel. 8. D's. 9. Fence. 10. Up. 11. On. 12. Son. 14. Headed. *Down:* 1. Piaffes. 2. Green. 3. Stale. 4. Wisp. 6. Neck. 8. Dun. 11. Old. 13. N.H.

**14.** Peter and Topper, Felicity and Sweet Kate, Christopher and Sundae, Tina and Blackbird.

**15.** 1. Both ways. 2. Gymkhana. 3. Yes. 4. Strangles. 5. Between 6 and 10 years. 6. Connemara. 7. 6 (throat lash buckle, 2 cheek strap buckles, 2 nose-band buckles, rein buckle). 8. Hackamore, which is a bitless bridle while the others are all kinds of bits. 9. False. 10. Blacksmith

**16.** 1. Heels, elbows. 2. White Horse Vale, grass. 3. Rider. 4. Horse, steed.

**17.** Aztec was the winner. He knocked three fences down and collected 12 faults. Benjamin knocked down four fences and collected 16 faults.

**18.** 1. A rug (cords attached to stop rug blowing up). 2. In the Knightsbridge Barracks, London. 3. Harness. 4. In the foot (a nail pressing on the sensitive part of the foot). 5. A curb chain (the lip strap passes through it). 6. Germany. 7. On a mouthing bit (pieces of metal to soften a young horse's mouth). 8. On the inside of the leg below the knee (injury caused by a blow from the opposite knee). 9. In the stomach. 10. On the end of the brush. 11. On the fetlock joint. 12. Spain (surefooted Iberian horses crossed with barbs).

**19.** 1. Horsemastership. 2. Thoroughbred. 3. Badminton. 4. Windsucker.

**20.** 1. A drink offered to riders at meets. 2. When the corn is cut between the end of July and September. 3. A white bodied hound with light yellow coloured markings. 4. They are not speaking when on the line of the fox. 5. A hunting tie. 6. They are baying outside the earth where the fox has just gone to ground. 7. A leash. 8. When a sheep or other animal crosses the line of the fox they foil the ground. 9. Cord or silk. 10. The fox has crossed the ride in a wood. 11. Flags. 12. A thruster.

**21.** *Across:* 1. Jumping. 5. As. 6. Colic. 7. Halt. 9. Ears. 11. Stable. 14. Shire. *Down:* 1. Jockey. 2. Molars. 3. Itch. 4. Gall. 8. Tread. 10. Star. 12. Bl. 13. h.h.

**22.** 1. Clydesdale. 2. Hippology. 5. Animalintex. 7. Mahogany tops. 9. Darley Arabian. 10. Kocholine. 11. Spurrier.

**23.** A. Body brush. B. Curry comb. C. Mane comb. D. Wisp. E. Water brush. F. Sweat scraper.

**24.** Paul did not groom Moonstone, nor did he give him time to digest the nuts. He stood in the middle of the hounds, instead of some way away with his pony's head turned towards them—the result was an injured hound. He failed to apologise for the mistake.

He then headed the fox by halloeing too soon and sent the fox back into the covert—an unforgivable sin in the hunting field.

25. 1. A type of veterinary poultice. 2. By dipping a piece of woollen cloth into hot water and disinfectant, bearable to the hand, and wrapping the cloth around the injured part. 3. Medicine or drugs made into a paste with treacle or honey smeared on the tongue, roof of the mouth, or back teeth. Good for sore throats. 4. Failure to dry the legs after washing and general neglect. 5. Keep the pony moving, reduce the feed and apply cold water to the feet. If it is severe, call the vet. 6. Bruises. 7. Stop the bleeding and clean the cut. 8. Rest the horse from the saddle and use salt and water to harden the skin. 9. Cold water. 10. Remove the nail which is pressing on the sensitive parts. 11. Clean out the foot and dress with boracic powder. 12. Treating parasitic skin diseases.

26. HEADCOLLAR. 1. Mash. 2. Mare. 3. Pedal bone. 4. Windsor. 5. Surcingle. 6. Palomino. 7. Ostler. 8. Vault. 9. Forage. 10. Carrots.

27. A. Arab. B. Barrel. C. Cat-hairs. D. Dray. E. Eel stripe. F. Ferrule. G. Gaucho. H. Hengest. I. Impulsion. J. Jockeys. K. Kimblewick. L. Lawn Meet.

28. 1. Manhattan (now renamed Jaegermester). 2. Buttevant Boy. 3. Foxhunter.

29. 1. London to York. 2. Morocco. 3. Sheila Wilcox. 4. Australia. 5. Black Agnes. 6. Winston. 7. Captain Mark Phillips. 8. Incitatus (he was a stallion and his name meant swift-speeding). 9. Trigger. 10. Lucinda Prior-Palmer.

30. 1. Headpiece. 2. Browband. 3. Cheek piece. 4. Noseband. 5. Snaffle bit. 6. Reins. 7. Martingale ring. 8. Martingale. 9. Neckstrap. 10. Throat lash.

31. *Across:* 1. Pony Club. 5. Bran. 6. Mules. 8. B.H.S. 9. Livery. 12. Year. 14. Sit. *Down:* 1. Pommel. 2. Nail.

3. Cobs. 4. Banks. 7. Eye. 8. Bye. 10. Vet. 11. Rye. 13. At.

**32.** 1. e, a, d, c, b. 2. d, b, c, a, e. 3. b, e, d, a, c.

**33.** 1. Piebald. 2. Black Bess. 3. The worst buckjumper in America. 4. Hilaire Belloc. 5. A polo pony. 6. Two of Mr. Jorrocks' hunters. 7. When driven Xerxes went in front of Arterxerxes. 8. Nimrod. 9. From Buenos Aires to Washington. 10. Boxer and Clover. 11. Black Beauty. 12. 600.

**34.** 1. Chestnut. 2. Dartmoor. 3. Piebald. 4. Hamstring. 5. Ringbone. 6. Headcollar.

**35.** 3. Gamgee should be used under bandages. 4. Witch-hazel lotion should be used to reduce swelling. 7. A colic drink is given when your horse has colic. 9. Kaolin paste should be used on swellings.

**36.** A and E are the same.

**37.** 1. A wrongly formed upper jaw, where the front teeth overhang the lower jaw. 2. In the corner of the eye. It is the third eyelid. 3. The hind leg lacks muscles and appears cut in above the hock. 4. A bone in the hind leg. 5. Knee. 6. On the lower part of each leg. 7. A horse's head with a convex profile line. 8. Eight true ribs, ten false. 9. Trachea. 10. Ham-string. 11. A finger or toe nail. 12. Bones at the back of the fetlock forming part of the joint.

**38.** 1. Always water your pony before feeding him. 2. A martingale stops the horse raising his head too high. 3. Give your horse plenty of hay in winter. 4. Pick out your pony's hooves every day. 5. Do not let your horse eat ragwort. 6. When hunting do not get in the hounds' way.

**40.** 1. Princess Anne. 2. Colonel Nigel Grove White. 3. Alvin Schockemöhle. 4. Richard III, at the Battle of Bosworth. 5. Fred Hartill. 6. Ginger McCain. 7. Marion Coakes. 8. Eddie Macken. 9. Anna Sewell. 10. Robert Smith. 11. Liz Edgar, married to Ted Edgar. 12. Prince Philip.

7. Kirkintilloch and Campsie. 8. Paddy McMahon and Penwood Forge Mill. 9. L'Escargot. 10. Harvey Smith and Salvador. 11. Caroline Bradley. 12. Hartwig Steenken.

41. *Across:* 1. Saddlery. 4. Gaskin. 6. View. 7. Bale. 9. Number. 10. Tail. 11. Cane. *Down:* 1. Spavin. 2. Draw. 3. Elk. 4. German. 5. Ill. 7. Bet. 8. Arab.

42. 1. Their armour was so heavy it was impossible for them to mount alone. 2. By putting the enchanted bit of a golden bridle in his mouth. 3. A light grey Arab. 4. a. 5. A grey thoroughbred from which all other grey thoroughbreds are developed. 6. To stop the horse lowering his head beyond a certain point. 7. 60 million years ago. 8. A war horse. 9. Western Mongolia. 10. Copenhagen. 11. The time of the Stuarts. 12. Extinct breeds of wild horses of the forest type.

43. 1. Hackney, hackamore. 2. Bâreme (French term for show jumping rules), barley, barrel, bardot (genet), bare-back, Barra pony (Highland breed), barrage (French term implying a jump off), Barouche (large open carriage). 3. Canter, cannon, cantle, canker. 4. Buckeroo, buckhounds, buck jumping, buckskin, bucket. 5. Forage, forehand, forelock, forge, forward seat. 6. Palomino, palfrey. 7. Windsucker, Windsor Greys, windgall. 8. New Zealand, New Forest, Newmarket.

44. 1. Yes. 2. Yes. 3. No, on the near side at the head. 4. No, hares. 5. Yes (he was a Greek writer). 6. No—they wind them. 7. Yes. 8. Yes. 9. No. 10. Yes. 11. No, it is one of the shire packs. 12. Yes.

45. 1. Stripe. 2. Star. 3. Snip. 4. Ermine Marks. 5. White stock.

46. 1. Shetland, New Forest, Dartmoor, Exmoor, Welsh Mountain, Connemara, Highland, Fell and Dale. 2. Westmoreland and Cumberland. 3. Mealy nose. 4. To carry heavy loads from the mines in the north.

5. Average height 40 inches (10 h.h.). 6. Highland. 7. Black, bay and brown. 8. Welsh Mountain, Welsh Cob and Welsh pony. 9. A pit pony. 10. The highlands of Scotland. 11. The Welsh Mountain. 12. Grey.

**47.** 1 and e, 2 and a, 3 and d, 4 and b, 5 and c.

**48.** 1. Jennet, hinny or bardot (offspring of a stallion and a female ass). 2. Donkey or eel stripe, list, ray. 3. Shin bone. 4. Stripe, rache or rase. 5. Speaks. 6. Chestnut roan. 7. Throat latch. 8. Coffin bone. 9. Pony gout, laminitis or fever in the feet. 10. Quarters-out (two track movement).

**49.** She is making four mistakes, her heels are up, her legs are too far back, her left rein is too long, and she is looking down. The horse's martingale is missing a strap and the bridle has no browband.

**50.** 1. Two time. 2. Flexing. 3. Nearside (left side). 4. To prevent the horse raising his head and therefore throwing the reins over his head. 5. Refuses to move forward. 6. Cane. 7. Dish. 8. Nutcracker action. 9. To raise the head. Yes, they should not be used. 10. Over the bit. 11. Suppling exercises to obtain better balance and obedience to the leg. Also improves collection. 12. Ordinary, collected, extended, disunited, counter.

**51.** 1. a. 2. a. 3. a.

**52.** 1. Quick release. 2. Job. 3. Sanfoin. 4. Pipe opener 5. Set-fair. 6. Heels. 7. Court. 8. Bone. 9. Sweating. 10. Shire.

**53.** 1. Steeplechase. 2. Appaloosa. 3. Martingale. 4. Pony Club.

**54.** 1. Wall, sole, white lines, bars, point and cleft of frog, seat of corn. 2. Rasping the front of the wall to shorten the toe. 3. Because the wall is insensitive with neither nerve nor blood supply. 4. Takes jar of impact, acts as shock absorber, and prevents slipping and concussion. 5. Drawing knife. 6. To keep the shoe in position and give greater security. 7. 3 on the inside and 4 on the outside. 8. To prevent brushing. 9. Cast shoe, loose shoe, shoe has worn thin, risen clench, overlong and out of shape foot. 10. Hunter shoe. To provide a better foothold and also for fitting nails through. 11. On the wall; it is a split. 12. Bruises of the sole beneath the heels of the shoe caused by badly fitted shoes and neglect of re-shoeing.

55. Air, ear, gait, gaiter, gate, grain, lame, laminae, lane, lariat, leg, ligament, line, lint, mane, mange, manger, mare, nag, nail, near, net, rail, rein, rig, ring, tag, tail, tar, team, tie, trail, train, trim.

56. 1. Highland ponies live wild in Scotland. 2. A stripe is a wide or narrow mark down the face. 3. Ponies are happier with a companion in the same field. 4. It is a good idea to lunge a new pony. 5. Horses are usually fond of sugar. 6. A horse should not be ridden a great deal when only four years old. 7. If your pony eats ragwort he will die. 8. The colour of a piebald is black and white. 9. A clipped horse should be stabled in winter. 10. A skip can be used instead of a wheelbarrow for mucking out.

57. 1. Trap (tail, rosette, anvil, plaits). 2. Fell (foal, ears, log, leg). 3. Whip (wisp, hay, iron, pony).

58. 1. German. 2. Italian. 3. American. 4. German. 5. Austrian. 6. Brazilian. 7. British. 8. German. 9. Italian. 10. British.

59. 1. Bay, brown, black, blue roan. 2. Snip, star, stripe. 3. Brownband, bit, bridoon, buckle. 4. Hock, hoof, head, heel, hamstring, hip. 5. Tendon, tail, throat, thigh. 6. Reversed oxer, rails, rustic post and rails, road closed. 7. Shire, Suffolk Punch, Shetland. 8. Carrots, corn, cubes, crushed oats. 9. Wisp, water brush. 10. Sprain, spavin, splint, sidebone.

**60.** 1. Jack ass. 2. Undershot. 3. Gee (call to turn right). 4. Hollow back. 5. Off. 6. Mare (entire is a stallion). 7. Roman nosed. 8. Switch tail. 9. Renvers (a two track movement, quarters out). 10. Sitting at the trot (posting means rising).

**61.** 1. Lorraine, Lorraine, Lorrèe by Charles Kingsley. 2. The Most Frightening Ride in History by Lord Byron.

**62.** 1. Two. 2. Four. 3. Twelve. 4. None. 5. Two. 6. Four (horny growths on fetlock joints). 7. Two. 8. Sixty-seven inches. 9. Two. 10. One pair. 11. Sixty-six feet. 12. One mile.

**63.** 1. 2,000 and 1,000 guineas, the Derby, Oaks, St. Leger. 2. 1780. 3. Henry VIII. 4. He broke a bone in his foot. 5. 30 m.p.h. 6. The last bend on the Epsom racecourse which is famous in the Derby. 7. Three times; in 1973, 1974 and 1977. 8. Colours on the jacket and cap worn by the jockeys. 9. January 1st. 10. 35 m.p.h. 11. King Flame. 12. John Francome.

**64/65.** GIANT CROSSWORD. *Across:* 1. Strangles. 6. Sit. 8. Turn. 9. Roller. 12. Rasps. 15. Treads. 16. Neigh. 18. Steed. 20. B.H.S. 22. Tent. 23. Dandy. 27. Girth. 29. Stalls. 30. Mealy. *Down:* 1. Shire. 2. Rail. 3. Nose. 4. Set. 5. Strap. 7. Irons. 10. Levade. 11. Drench. 13. Snip. 14. Trot. 17. Hunt. 18. Sly. 19. Dun. 20. Bay. 21. Stripe. 24. Arab. 25. Dale. 26. Ass. 28. Hay.

**66.** 1. Irish martingale. 2. Blacksmith's pincers. 3. Drawing knife. 4. Leather punch. 5. Fly fringe. 6. Buffer.

**67.** 1. Flying change. 2. Opening meet. 3. Over faced. 4. Road closed. 5. Full mouth. 6. Racing seat. 7. Stirrup tread. 8. White face. 9. Drop fence. 10. Girth gall. 11. Neck strap. 12. Tail guard.

**68.** Pictures 2 and 3 are the same.

**69.** 1. A large, plain, ugly shaped head. 2. Heavy breeds and most cross breeds. 3. Frost nails. 4. Spurs. 5. A hunting term used when the ground is muddy and cut up in front of a jump. 6. The National Pony Stud Book. 7. Give a horse a light groom without removing the rugs completely. 8. Big round hooves which are out of proportion and low on the heel. 9. Rowel. 10. By coiling a piece of rope, hay or straw in the form of a figure of eight to make a pad. 11. Conformation. 12. A four-wheeled vehicle for breaking horses.

**70.** 1. Browband, paddock, foxhunt, stringhalt (nervous disease affecting hind legs), piebald, forelock, Dartmoor. 2. Highland, dressage, sandcrack, bullfinch, noseband, blacksmith, gaskin.

**71.** *Across:* 1. Trekking. 5. Nag. 6. Coat. 8. Oaks. 10. Oats. 11. Colt. 13. Trot. 14. Rug. *Down:* 1. Tendon. 2. Ergot. 3. Kick. 4. Gates. 7. Ostler. 9. Ascot. 12. Br.

**72.** Mane comb, brass polish, kitchen knife, wisp, cooking oil, washing up liquid.

**73.** A. Foxglove. B. Yew. C. Deadly nightshade. D. Ragwort. E. Hemlock. F. Ivy.

**74.** 1. The American quarter horse. 2. Cutting pony. 3. Lope. 4. Chaps. 5. Cinch. 6. Fitting on the front of American saddles used for roping. 7. Bosal noseband. 8. A gelding with a quarter horse build and a pinto colouring. 9. The high tail carriage. 10. Roached. 11. Terms used in buck jumping. Jack knifing is when the front and the hind legs click together while in the air. Sunfishing is when the body is twisted into a crescent. 12. Lariat.

**75.** 1. b. 2. a. 3. d. 4. b. 5. d. 6. b.

**76.** 1. Walter de la Mare. 2. Rudyard Kipling. 3. The Revelation of St. John the Divine (chapter 6, verse 2). 4. Samuel Johnson (oats). 5. R. S. Surtees (famous sporting author whose most famous work was *Jorrocks' Jaunts and Jollities.*)

**77.** Stable: this is the only item not beginning with B, (the others are: brush, bit, bucket, and boot).

**78.** 1. Fetlock. 2. Lipizzaner. 3. Martingale. 4. Capriole. 5. Showjumping. 6. Skewbald. 7. Grand National. 8. Palomino. 9. Harness. 10. Trotting. 11. Cavalletti. 12. Breeding.

**79.** *Across:* 1. Show. 3. Cap. 5. Incisors. 7. Pit. 8. Flank. 9. In. 10. Bone. 11. Bar. *Down:* 1. Sainfoin. 2. Whinny. 3. Crop. 4. Post. 6. Riding. 10. br.

**80.** 1. Lameness and pointing of the foot to rest it. 2. In the heel region. 3. Shoe boil. 4. Because the swelling could be pushed from one side of the hock to the other (the swelling is fluid distension). 5. A soft painful swelling between the ears due to a blow or pressure from a headcollar. 6. By not reducing the feed when your horse is not working. He will drag his hindlegs and hardly be able to move. 7. Stringhalt. 8. Lice. 9. On the back in the saddle region. 10. An abrasion of the skin behind the pastern or the knee, caused by getting caught up in a rope or chain. 11. Roaring or whistling. 12. At the back of the knee joint.

**81.** First of all Jill and her father bought a pony in a hurry—something you must never do. They bought him from a sale without knowing him and without being experts—a fundamental mistake. They bought a three year old which was too young to be ridden. They also bought him without the help of someone knowledgeable and without a vet's certificate. Jill rode Cavalier as soon as he arrived and didn't give him time to settle down. Jill and her father made all these mistakes and bought a rogue.

**82.** 1. David Broome. 2. Geoffrey Glazzard. 3. Caroline Bradley. 4. Debbie Johnsey. 5. Harvey Smith. 6. Eddie Macken. 7. Mike Saywell. 8. Liz Edgar. 9. Malcolm Pyrah. 10. Graham Fletcher.

**84.** 1. Three refusals: starting before the bell: disobedience for more than one minute: showing an obstacle to the horse before starting: unauthorised assistance: not crossing the finishing line mounted: not going through the start or through the finish. 2. His head should come up and his neck shorten. 3. £150–300. 4. At the end of the 1800s. 5. Princess Anne. 6. The same distance as the height of the fence or half as much again. 7. Special adult events for Grade C horses ridden by members of the B.S.J.A. Named after the great international show-jumper. 8. Douglas Bunn. 9. Quite fast because it is a spread fence. 10. A three-day combined training event. 11. A double oxer has a pole on each side of a brush fence while an oxer only has one on the take-off side. 12. A training method used to make a horse jump higher. As he goes over a jump, a pole is raised so that he hits his hind legs and is therefore 'rapped'.

**85.** 1. George Stubbs. 2. Sporting pictures. 3. Munnings. 4. You would usually have to jump small drums, which are removed one by one until you are eliminated for failing to jump them. 5. Strathblane Pony Club. 6. No. You may enter open events. 7. $7\frac{1}{2}$ minutes. 8. Mallet. 9. In the mid-nineteenth century. 10. 300 yards.

**86.** 1. Yes. 2. Yes. 3. No. The pace they travel along the road. 4. Yes. 5. No. When they use their voices after they know the fox is in covert. 6. Yes. 7. Yes. 8. No. It is soaked and boiled. 9. No. The width of the leg below the knee is less than the measurement just above the fetlock. 10. Yes. 11. No. To smarten and improve the neck and for refinement. 12. Yes.

**87.** *Across:* 1. Roller. 5. Ear. 6. Bone. 7. Sole. 10. Mustangs. 11. At. 12. Grass. *Down:* 1. Ribs. 2. Land. 3. Remounts. 4. Breeds. 8. Cut. 9. Star. 10. May.

**88.** 1. National Equestrian Centre. 2. Master of Foxhounds Association. 3. National Pony Society. 4. Horse of the Year Show. 5. Riding Club. 6. Riding for the Disabled. 7. bl. 8. fav. 9. c. 10. 14 h.h. 11. t.b. 12. f.

**89.** 1. Highland. 2. Connemara. 3. Dartmoor. 4. Shetland. 5. Fell. 6. Exmoor.

**90.** Bee Line was the winner. Then came Likely Lad, Father's Folly, Oxford Blue, Westward Ho, Lightning Streak, Hurry Harry, Tornado, Flying Dutchman, and Winalot in last place.

**91.** 1. Wheat. It is the waste product from flour milling. 2. A non-gall girth. It is split into three and gives the horse's forelegs more room. 3. It is too prickly. 4. To avoid pressure on the spine. The horse is less likely to get cast in the stable. 5. 56 lbs. 6. Burning cat hairs off a horse's coat. 7. Stainless steel, nickel, vulcanite, rubber. 8. The short pieces of hay tend to fall through the haynet and get wasted. 9. All the coat except for the saddle patch and the legs down from the shoulders and thighs. 10. Tying the horse up very short to a ring in the stable. 11. A ventilation window that opens inwards. 12. Stops the horse bolting his food and helps him grind up his food and, of course, increases the feed.

**92.** 1. Strangles. 2. Capped elbow. 3. Broken knee. 4. Sidebone. 5. Sprained tendon. 6. Girth gall. 7. Slipped stifle. 8. Bone spavin. 9. Windgall. 10. Curb. 11. Saddle sore. 12. Poll evil.

**93.** 1. d. 2. c. 3. a. 4. c. 5. a. 6. d.

**94.** 1. An eggbutt snaffle. 2. The frog. 3. A standing martingale. 4. The old line of a fox. 5. A horse's ribs. 6. A ewe neck. 7. A covert or a hound can be drawn from the pack. 8. A horse stumbling. 9. When it is the followers of a hunt. 10. In the saddle (rising at the trot).

**95.** M. Music. N. Nutcracker action. O. Odd coloured. P. Pirouette. Q. Quiddor. R. Rasp. S. Shafts. T. Tucked up. U. Undershot. V. Volt. W. Whelps. X. Xerxes. Y. Yawing. Z. Zebra stripes.

**96.** 1. Pelham (correct). 2. Hindquarters are goose-rumped (a fault). 3. Standing martingale has no neck strap. 4. Sausage boot (correct). 5. Hunting whip has no lash. 6. Tail guard (correct).

**97.** 1. Jane Bullen (at Mexico in 1968). 2. Newmarket Racecourse. 3. Richard Walker on Pasha in 1969. 4. Marion Mould on Stroller. 5. Sixty-six. 6. 1912. 7. 18·2 h.h. 8. Sheila Wilcox. 9. Pat Smythe. 10. Two minutes, eight seconds.

**98.** 1. Shire and anvil. 2. Hunting and crest. 3. Stripe and manger. 4. Polo and saddlery. 5. Rasp and snaffle. 6. Drench and oats.

**99.** 1. Canter/trance. 2. Cats/cast. 3. Stripe/priest. 4. Polo/loop. 5. Lame/meal. 6. Rear/rare. 7. Dale/lead. 8. Girth/right. 9. Lope/pole. 10. Astride/tirades.

**100.** 1 Four toes in front, three behind. 2. A Russian breed of horse. 3. At the artery on the inside of the forelimb below the elbow joint, or the artery of the round bone of the lower jaw. 4. £75 or over. 5. Courbette. 6. An Indian groom. 7. Mesohippus, Pliohippus and Merychippus. 8. The horse is flexing and bending at the poll with his nose dipped downwards. 9. In front of the molar teeth. 10. Andrew Fielder. 11. A sulky. 12. It is a dressage term referring to the rhythm and tempo of a horse's paces. The movement should always be regular and symmetrical.

If you have enjoyed this book, you will find lots more titles in Armada's Pony Parade to give you hours of exciting reading.
Find out more about the wonderful range of pony books Armada has to offer, on the following pages.

# Pony Care from A-Z

by Charlotte Popescu
Illustrated by Christine Bousfield

What is a hackamore? How much should you feed a pony? How should you treat a girth gall? How can you tell a horse's age?

The answers to these, and a thousand other questions, can be found in this fact-filled encyclopedia, together with all you need to know about grooming, feeding, ailments, tack, grazing and stabling.

An invaluable, pocket-sized handbook—easy to look up and with scores of clear illustrations. A mine of information and helpful hints for all pony-lovers.

# Good Riding

by Christine Pullein-Thompson

Illustrated by Christine Bousfield

Christine Pullein-Thompson, famous for her popular pony novels, takes you step by step from your first riding lesson to that thrilling first clear round.

With illustrations on every page, *Good Riding* covers mounting, your hands, your seat, the aids, pace and control, schooling, hacking, learning to jump, coping with problems, tack—and more ambitious activities like pony clubbing, hunting, show jumping, gymkhanas, etc.

Learn to ride well, from the very beginning, and discover for yourself the excitement and fun to be found in that very special partnership—a good rider on a well-schooled pony.

## DIANA PULLEIN-THOMPSON

A PONY TO SCHOOL
THREE PONIES AND SHANNAN
*Two more exciting pony books by Diana Pullein-Thompson*

### THREE PONIES AND SHANNAN

Christina Carr has everything most girls dream of: rich parents, a beautiful home with a butler and cook, an Irish Wolfhound puppy called Shannan, and three prize-winning ponies. She should be completely happy. But she isn't. She's lonely, and longs to make friends with the noisy village children on their rough, unschooled ponies. They, however, despise her.

How Christina stops being a spoilt little rich girl, goes to riding club camp and makes a friend for life is an engrossing and thrilling pony story.

### A PONY TO SCHOOL

*The sequel to Three Ponies and Shannan*

Christina and her friend Augusta are asked to school the skewbald pony, Clown. He is nervous and difficult, but they are determined to turn him into a happy, obedient mount. Then they discover why Clown's previous owners have failed to control him. The skewbald is a rearer – and if Christina and Augusta can't cure him of his dreadful habit, he will have to be destroyed ...

Armada

# JOSEPHINE PULLEIN-THOMPSON

### SIX PONIES
### PONY CLUB TEAM
### ONE DAY EVENT
### PONY CLUB CAMP

Meet the members of the West Barsetshire Pony Club and read about their riding adventures and hilarious escapades in four favourite books by Josephine Pullein-Thompson.

### SIX PONIES

The Pony Club members face the exciting challenge of breaking in six New Forest ponies – and Noel earns a pony of her own.

### PONY CLUB TEAM

The Major makes a bet that his team will win at the Pony Club Hunter Trials, and runs a special training course for them. But with the Trials only a few days away, their riding is still hopeless...

### ONE DAY EVENT

A great day for the Pony Club – and Noel is determined to prove that Sonnet is good enough to win...

### PONY CLUB CAMP

It's the high spot of the summer – as children and ponies arrive in glorious confusion at Folly Court to begin a week in camp. And there are some exciting surprises in store for them...

Armada

# CHRISTINE PULLEIN-THOMPSON

### PHANTOM HORSE
### PHANTOM HORSE COMES HOME
### PHANTOM HORSE GOES TO IRELAND

The three thrilling books by Christine Pullein-Thompson about Phantom, the beautiful, wild palomino whom no one could capture.

## PHANTOM HORSE
The story of how Angus and Jean Hamilton go to America, and catch their first glimpse of Phantom in the Blue Ridge Mountains. They are determined to catch him – but so are others, whose motives are sinister . . .

## PHANTOM HORSE COMES HOME
Phantom is now Jean's greatest joy, but wildness is still in his blood – and when the family has to move back to England, Jean knows he'll never stand the plane journey. Halfway across the Atlantic, Phantom goes mad . . .

## PHANTOM HORSE GOES TO IRELAND
A trip to Killarney with Phantom and Angus will be a wonderful holiday, Jean imagines. But it is not the peaceful place she expects. Strange noises are heard in their host's house at night – and then Angus is kidnapped . . .

Armada

# 'JINNY AT FINMORY' BOOKS
### *by Patricia Leitch*

FOR LOVE OF A HORSE

A DEVIL TO RIDE

THE SUMMER RIDERS
*Armada Originals*

Meet red-haired, rebellious Jinny Manders and her chestnut Arab mare, Shantih, in Armada's newest pony series.

### FOR LOVE OF A HORSE
The Manders family moves from the city to a new life in Scotland, and Jinny's dream of owning a horse seems about to come true when she rescues Shantih from a cruel circus. But Shantih escapes on to the moors where Jinny despairs of ever getting near her – and she knows the Arab will never survive the highland winter . . .

### A DEVIL TO RIDE
Shantih, safe, for the first time in her life, in the Manders' stable, comes to love her new mistress almost as much as Jinny adores the beautiful mare. But Shantih is impossible to ride, and Jinny can't control her . . .

### THE SUMMER RIDERS
Jinny is furious when Marlene, the brash city girl, comes to stay and insists on riding Shantih. But when Marlene's brother, Bill, gets into trouble with the local police, Jinny and Shantih are the only ones who can help Marlene to stop him being prosecuted.

Armada

# CAPTAIN ARMADA

## has a whole shipload of exciting books for you

Armadas are chosen by children all over the world. They're designed to fit your pocket, and your pocket money too. They're colourful, gay, and there are hundreds of titles to choose from. Armada has something for everyone:

Mystery and adventure series to collect, with favourite characters and authors – like Alfred Hitchcock and The Three Investigators. The Hardy Boys. Young detective Nancy Drew. The intrepid Lone Piners. Biggles. The rascally William – and others.

Hair-raising spinechillers – ghost, monster and science fiction stories. Super craft books. Fascinating quiz and puzzle books. Lots of hilarious fun books. Many famous children's stories. Thrilling pony adventures. Popular school stories – and many more exciting titles which will all look wonderful on your bookshelf.

You can build up your own Armada collection – and new Armadas are published every month, so look out for the latest additions to the Captain's cargo.

If you'd like a complete, up-to-date list of Armada books, send a stamped, self-addressed envelope to:

Armada Books,
14 St James's Place,
London SW1A 1PF